Under th

Written by Jo Windsor

Rigby

Look under the ground. Look at the worms.

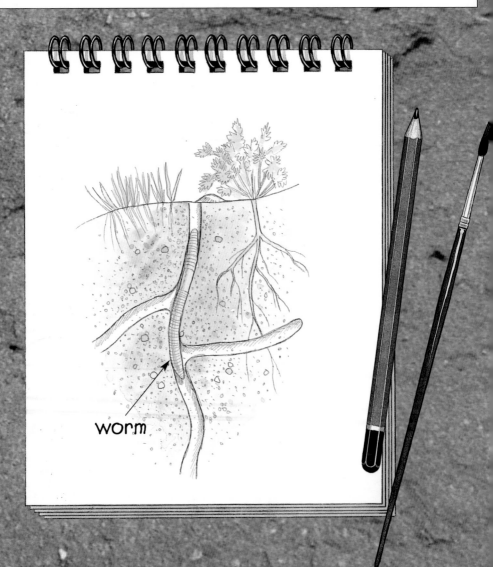

worm

Look under the ground.
Look at the mole.

mole

Look under the ground.
Look at the fox.

fox

Look under the ground.
Look at the ants.

ant

Look under the ground.
Look at the rabbit.

rabbit

Look under the ground.

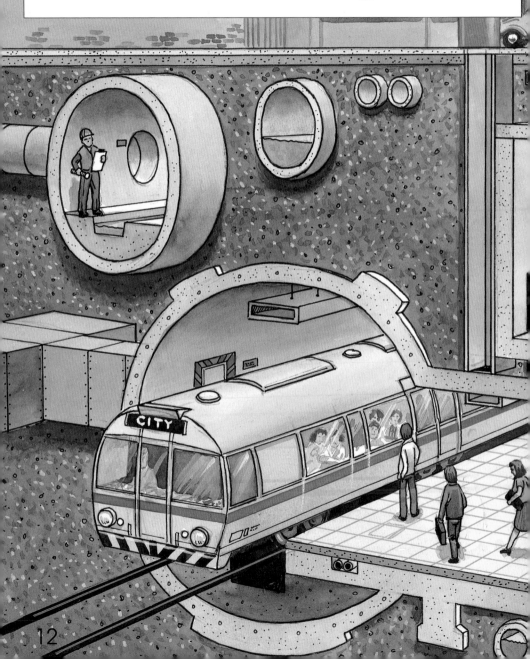

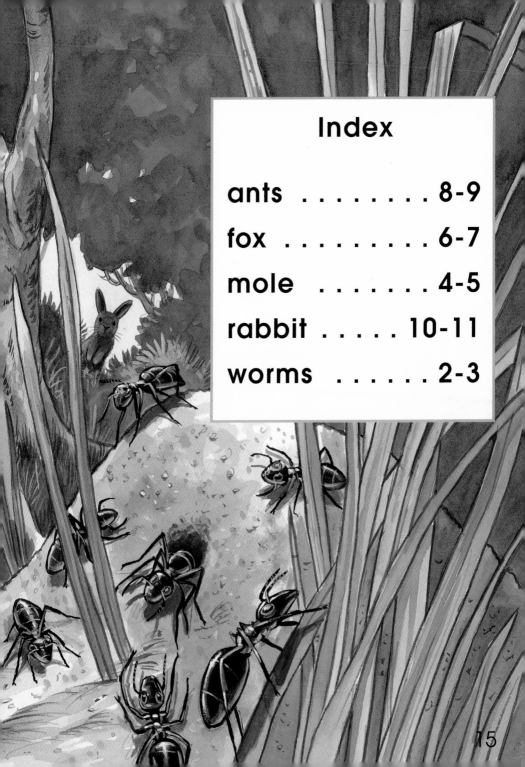

Index

▬▬ Guide Notes

Title: Under the Ground

Stage: Emergent – Magenta

Genre: Nonfiction

Approach: Guided Reading

Processes: Thinking Critically, Exploring Language, Processing Information

Written and Visual Focus: Photographs (static images), Illustrations, Index

Word Count: 44

READING THE TEXT

Tell the children that this book is about some animals that live under the ground.
Talk to them about what is on the front cover. Read the title and the author.
Focus the children's attention on the index and talk about the animals that are in this book.
"Walk" through the book, focusing on the photographs, and talk about the different animals.
Read the text together.

THINKING CRITICALLY
(sample questions)
- What other things can live under the ground?
- Why do the animals in this book live under the ground?

EXPLORING LANGUAGE
(ideas for selection)

Terminology
Title, cover, author, photographs, illustrations

Vocabulary
Interest words: fox, ants, mole, rabbit, worms, ground
High-frequency words: look, at, the
Positional word: under